Helping Your Toddler to Sleep

an easy-to-follow guide

Siobhan Mulholland

Vermilion

Contents

Introduction

So much happens during the toddler years – the change that occurs between a 12-month-old and a 36-month-old is huge. A one-year-old may just be attempting to stand up in preparation for his first steps; a three-year-old will be running around like a mad thing. Likewise on his first birthday your child may be able to say the odd, short word; on his third birthday he'll be able to describe a simple event. Your child's development will be rapid, so fast that at some point during the toddler years his sleep is bound to be affected: he may sleep more, he may sleep less, he may wake more often, go to bed later, wake up earlier. There are many variables. This book will guide you through most of them and help you to work towards having a toddler who sleeps well both during the night and the day.

Please note that to avoid confusion the toddler has always been referred to as 'he' but this could just as easily have been 'she'.

Chapter 1

SLEEP The facts and figures

Toddlers sleep much like the rest of us – they toss and turn, they twitch, they move about, they dream, they have nightmares, they murmur, and they wake up and fall asleep again several times a night. But there is one big difference between toddlers and the rest of us – and that is that they need many more hours of sleep. It's essential for their development, growth and wellbeing. A toddler who's had too little sleep is not a pretty sight – he may be agitated, cranky, perhaps even overexcited. That's why making sure your toddler gets the right amount of sleep during the night – and day – is so important.

HOW TODDLERS SLEEP

A lot goes on during those night-time hours. While we slumber our bodies do not shut down. We are not cut off from the outside world – we remain conscious of our surroundings. How light the room is, how hot or cold, how noisy or quiet: it all has an effect on us while we sleep. We will sense it if we become hungry or uncomfortable. This is because sleep is an active, organised physiological process that requires energy.

Sleep cycles

When your toddler sleeps it is not in one continuous state. He doesn't lay his head down on the pillow, shut his eyes, drift off and stay like that for the best part of the night. What happens is he drifts in and out of different types and states of sleep – from light sleep to deep sleep and back again in cycles. In the same way as an adult does, throughout the night, your toddler will alternate between being drowsy and almost awake, to being so deeply asleep that it's almost impossible to rouse him.

By analysing brain waves scientists have been able to identify which type of sleep we're experiencing and when. They have broken sleep down into different categories and – depending on what time you go to bed, during the night or day – it is possible to pinpoint the times you will experience different states of sleep.

We drift in and out of these different types of sleep in a set pattern, in a predictable cycle. Each sleep 'cycle' lasts a set amount of time. In adults it takes around 90 minutes, but for children these sleep cycles are shorter – around 50 minutes, so a toddler will hit the heights and depths of sleep much more quickly than an adult. However, as your child gets older his sleep cycle will get progressively longer and by the time he's an adolescent he'll have the same length of cycle as you.

States of sleep

Sleep is categorised into two main types or 'states'. They are referred to as 'light' sleep and 'deep' sleep, also known as REM (Rapid Eye Movement) sleep and non-REM sleep. It's these two states of sleep that we are 'cycling' through during the night.

REM sleep

REM sleep is the state of sleep closest to wakefulness. In babies it is referred to as 'active sleep' because it's when our physiological systems are most active. Toddlers experience a lot more REM sleep than adults.

While in REM sleep we are more 'vigilant', more conscious of what's going on, and we rouse more easily. This is when adults are more likely to wake up because of certain, specific noises. For instance, you may sleep through an early-morning plane flying overhead, but will waken as soon as you hear your toddler crying in his cot. For children and infants it's not so much noise that will wake them up as hunger and discomfort. So your toddler may sleep through thunder, lightning and the pounding of torrential rain, but if he's hungry or thirsty he'll wake up and no doubt make sure you do as well.

What happens when your toddler experiences REM sleep

- Your child's eyelids will be closed but his eyes occasionally appear to move from side to side beneath his lids. Even adults experiencing REM sleep can be seen to move their eyes back and forth beneath their eyelids (which explains the term Rapid Eye Movement).
- Your toddler uses up more energy and oxygen when experiencing REM sleep.
- Your toddler may twitch and jerk in his sleep.
- His breathing and heartbeat will become irregular.
- This is when older children and adults dream. Your one-year-old may be dreaming as well, but as infants can't tell us we don't know for sure. However, as soon as your toddler is speaking – probably from around two years old – he may start talking about his dreams.

Non-REM sleep

At 12 months of age, every time his head hits that pillow and he closes his eyes, your child's sleep cycles will start with a period of non-REM sleep.

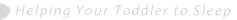

Non-REM sleep is divided up into a further four stages varying progressively from drowsiness to very deep sleep.

Stage 1: The lightest sleep – the half-and-half stage between wakefulness and sleep. Your toddler may be drowsy and you'll see his eyes droop and slowly close. If he's sitting up or strapped in his car seat it's when his head dramatically falls forward or to one side as he starts nodding off.

Stage 2: A very light sleep. Your toddler's breathing pattern and heart rate will start to slow, and he will be quiet and still. He will wake easily at this stage, so a sudden, loud noise may give him a fright.

Stage 3: Your toddler will be in a very deep sleep and will not move.

Stage 4: Your toddler's breathing and heart rate will be at their lowest levels because he is very deeply asleep. It will be very difficult to wake him: you can move him into his cot, change him into pyjamas, possibly even have builders knocking the house down and he's likely to sleep through it all. Your toddler achieves this very deep state of sleep within minutes of closing his eyes. He races through the lighter stages of non-REM to get there, whereas adults only pass through these stages gradually. On reaching this comatose-like state your child will then pass through each stage again, in reverse order, before drifting into a state of REM sleep.

**What happens when
your toddler experiences
non-REM sleep**

- His heart rate lowers –
  he will have a more
  regular heart rate.
- His breathing slows
  down; he breathes
  deeply and lies very still.
- His muscles relax.
- He will be difficult to wake up.
- We know from older children and adults that very
  little dreaming happens during this state.

Cycling in Your Sleep

The fact that your toddler has a more 'rapid' sleep cycle than you is significant. Adults and young children alike start their cycles off with a period of non-REM sleep followed by a period of REM sleep. However, as we come to the end of each period of REM sleep, we wake up slightly – we undergo a moment of arousal. We may move about, adjust our position in bed, and subconsciously check to see that everything is as it should be.

In adults these moments of arousal happen around five times a night. For most of us it's not a problem; after these few seconds – or sometimes even minutes – of relative alertness, we quickly doze off again. We don't wake up all the way unless something out of the ordinary disturbs us such as a noise or being in a different environment. We will not remember this brief period of wakefulness and it has little effect on how we feel the next day. But it's different for your toddler: not only is he experiencing more cycles of REM sleep than you, a state of sleep from which he could be easily awakened, but his sleep cycles are also shorter, bringing more moments of arousal and potential wakening.

If your toddler has yet to learn how to doze off again without any help from you, then this is when he will wake up fully and cry out for assistance. And in many ways he couldn't really choose a worse moment: given that your sleep cycles are not in synch he will probably disturb you when you are very deeply asleep and this will make you feel tired and groggy the following day.

However, although you may feel it's not exactly a win-win situation, it does get better. As your toddler matures, so does his sleep cycle. His cycle will grow longer and he will experience less REM sleep, so – with maybe a little help from you – he should wake up less frequently as he gets older, and need less help from you to get back to sleep again.

HOW MUCH SLEEP YOUR TODDLER NEEDS

How long is a piece of string? We are all different and we all have different sleep needs. Some adults appear to thrive on four or five hours of sleep a night, others can't function on less than eight. Trying to work out how much sleep your toddler needs is a bit like adapting a recipe to make a cake – tinkering around the edges to get it just right. The vast majority of children fall somewhere within the averages listed on the chart overleaf. You may find your toddler needs an hour more or less at night, or perhaps an extra half-hour for his naps. You know your toddler better than anyone else, so you are the best judge of this.

12 months old

By his first birthday, your toddler will still need around 11 hours' sleep a night and 2½ hours' sleep during the day. He may still be having two naps a day: one in the morning and one in the afternoon lasting 1– 1½ hours each in duration. However, it's around the time of their first birthday that some toddlers start showing signs of needing less sleep during the day. If you think your child is in this category then he may be ready to just have one long nap after lunch each day.

As your one-year-old becomes more active he will be more ready for sleep at nap times and bedtime. However, his increased mobility may mean it takes longer to get him to lie down and go to sleep in his cot. This is the age when many toddlers first discover they can stand up by pulling themselves up with the help of the bars on their cots. Getting back down, though, is a different thing – often needing your help.

18 months old

Until their second birthday toddlers need around 13 hours of sleep over a 24-hour period. The norm is for around 11 hours at night. Most toddlers still need two naps a day at a year old, but by the time they're 18 months old they are usually ready for just a single nap. This usually happens after lunch, in the early afternoon, and lasts between one and a half and two hours.

24 months old

By his second birthday your toddler will still be sleeping around 10– 11 hours a night, with a nap of 1– 2 hours after lunch. Sleep disturbances, such as nightmares and sleep walking, start to become apparent from two years of age but are something that most children eventually grow out of.

This is the age when your previously perfect sleeper may well start to be a little challenging. At nap times and bedtime he may try very hard to keep himself awake, even when he is tired. He may refuse to lie down, to stop talking; in fact he may use all his new-found developmental skills to resist sleep.

At around 2½ years many children come out of nappies during the day. Some parents attempt nights without nappies at this age, which can cause sleep disruption.

36 months old

From the age of three to adolescence, children need gradually less and less sleep. Once children are past the toddler age they rarely nap and they slowly begin to sleep less at night.

SLEEP CHART
Average number of hours of sleep over a 24-hour period
These figures are average amounts and will differ from child to child. Your child should be getting around the total number of hours in the third column, but how you divide that up is down to you and your child.

Age (months)	Total Night-time Sleep (hours)	Total Daytime Sleep (hours)	Total Number (hours)
12	11	2–3	13–14
18	11	$1^1/_2$–$2^1/_2$	13–14
24	10–11	1–2	12–13
36	10–11	0–$1^1/_2$	12–13

It's around this age that many children begin nursery. When it comes to sleep this is usually a very good thing. Young children initially find nursery very tiring, which means they are more than ready to go to bed at night and tend to sleep very well indeed.

NAPS
It can be hard to strike the right balance in terms of how long your toddler should sleep during the day. If he naps for too long then he'll have trouble getting to sleep at bedtime and may not sleep through. But if you cut down too much on naps, you'll have an over-tired toddler who is irritable when awake and has difficulty settling to sleep.

And, of course, toddlers' napping needs can vary greatly. One might seem none the worse for missing a nap, while another might turn into a grouchy horror. You know best what sort of toddler you have, and will work out what is best for him.

HOW TO TELL IF YOUR TODDLER IS NOT GETTING ENOUGH SLEEP

It's quite hard – the above figures are averages and very few children thrive on anything drastically different to this, but number-crunching may not be the best way to gauge if your toddler is getting enough sleep. What can be a more accurate indicator is how your child behaves when he is awake – his ability to concentrate, how many tantrums he has, and what his 'moods' are like during the day. Here are some behaviour traits to look out for:

- A very obvious one – he yawns a lot and rubs his eyes.
- Sluggish and whiney. Your toddler struggles to keep awake during the day; he is obviously tired, a tad irritable and appears listless.
- Tantrums and tears. All toddlers have tantrums, some more than others, and to a certain extent that's the luck of the draw – some toddlers are predisposed to rant a lot. However, lack of sleep will certainly worsen those supermarket-queue or mealtime outbreaks.
- Co-ordination. Lack of sleep affects co-ordination in all of us. You may notice your toddler's hand-to-eye co-ordination suffers; he's less able to build bricks or put the correct shape through the right hole. Or, your toddler may appear clumsier, falling over and spilling or dropping things.
- Sociability. Toddlers who aren't getting enough shuteye are more likely to be withdrawn and less sociable. They may play on their own and if they do join in with others it often ends in tears.
- Hyperactivity. Sleep deprivation often goes unnoticed because it can actually cause over-activity in a toddler. Your child may appear as if he has lots of energy, he may seek constant stimulation and be unable to concentrate on anything for very long.

HOW TO TELL IF YOUR TODDLER IS GETTING ENOUGH SLEEP

Your toddler will fall asleep quickly, he will sleep well when he is asleep, and he'll wake up easily and be in a pleasant mood. During the day he'll only nap the average amount for his age and be wide awake and full of energy.

Chapter 2

WHAT IT TAKES FOR YOUR TODDLER
to have a good night's sleep

Young children are most secure when they know who's who and what's what. They thrive on routine and daily structure; the unexpected, however exciting, always seems to end in upset. Consistency and security is what they seek, so make sure that how they go about getting to sleep differs little each night – that they are in the same bed or cot, in the same room, that they have their favourite bedding and that bedtime happens at the same time each evening. But, most important of all, make sure the events leading up to 'lights out' differ little on a daily basis. The formula is simple: bath, book, bed.

WHERE IS YOUR TODDLER GOING TO SLEEP?

In a cot

This is what you probably put your toddler in when he was a baby and many parents see no reason to change this until their child is around three years old. At around 12 months old toddlers often start enjoying their new-found mobility. They roll around; they pull themselves up to stand and fall over a lot. That's why a cot works – it's a safe place that younger toddlers cannot fall (or clamber) out of.

In a bed

Although many a bed manufacturer may try to convince you that only the best for your toddler will do, there's also many a sleep expert will tell you that all of us – especially young children – quickly get used to whatever we're sleeping on. It usually only takes one night – two at the most – for us to adjust to whatever surface or type of bed we're in. So don't worry about splashing out on a top-of-the-range product. Something clean and comfy is all that matters.

That said, if you are going to buy a new bed for your toddler a lower one is, in the short term, the safest. This is one that is quite near to the ground so if your toddler falls out (and they are prone to) he doesn't have so far to fall. Some children's 'starter beds' come with adjustable guard rails – they're a bit like a cross between a cot and a bed, so you may want to try this option if you are worried about your toddler injuring himself. See pages 24–5 for moving your toddler from a cot to a bed.

With you

Whether children should sleep in the same bed as their parents or not is a topic that has attracted much debate. There are plenty of arguments for and against, and plenty of parents passionate on both sides of the argument. This is very much your personal decision – a choice to be made along the grounds of what suits you, your child, your partner and your family.

TOP TIP
If you opt for co-sleeping, the bigger the bed, the easier it will be. So think really big, think King Size, and you're all likely to sleep a lot better.

Pro:

- If your child is a very light sleeper who wakes up easily and often, then he may be reassured sleeping in the same bed as you. Whenever he rouses he can see and feel your presence.
- Having your toddler sleeping next to you can be easier for you. When he wakes at night either for a feed, or seeking comfort, you're on hand to help; you don't need to get out of bed so your sleep is less disturbed.
- Being in close proximity with your child throughout the night can be very comforting for both parent and child, providing lots of physical contact.

Con:

- If your child is used to having you by his side all night, every night, he will find it much more difficult to become an independent sleeper – one who can settle himself, who can roll over and fall asleep again without your help or presence. So when it comes to encouraging your toddler to sleep in his own bed, it may take longer than if he started out in the beginning in his own cot.
- Your toddler has a different sleep cycle to you, so when he rouses at the end of each of his sleep cycles it is at a different time to when you will rouse. If you are in your deepest moments of sleep it can be painful to say the least.
- Toddlers by their very nature are active. They are active during the day and surprisingly active when they sleep as well. They toss and turn and twist around, and they have little respect for which bit of the bed belongs to whom.

WARNING
Never have your toddler sleeping with you if you or any other person in the bed is a smoker, even if you never smoke in bed; if you have drunk alcohol; or if you have taken any drug (legal or illegal) that could make you extra sleepy.

- You may find you sleep very lightly with your toddler next to you – you may be 'conscious' of him all the time, afraid of disturbing him. This could affect the quality of your sleep.

Many parents decide on a compromise – having their toddler sleep in his own cot or bed for most of the night, but letting him join them for an early-morning cuddle.

TEMPERATURE

Young children sleep better in a cooler environment – if your toddler's bedroom is too warm he will have difficulty getting to sleep and staying asleep. He's more likely to wake up in the night if he's too hot rather than too cold.

So aim for a 'cool' room – one where the temperature is around 18 degrees Celsius (64°F). This will probably be a lot cooler than you think or are used to, so keep a thermometer in your child's room to monitor the temperature.

Most importantly, your toddler should never sleep with a hot-water bottle or electric blanket, or next to a radiator, heater or fire.

BEDDING

Because it's so vital for your child not to overheat, the type of bedding he sleeps in is also important. Stick to sheets, blankets and covers made of cotton and wool, as these dissipate heat more easily than bedding made of artificial fibres. And do take note of the tog rating of your toddler's covers – this is the system used to indicate the warmth of duvets, quilts and sleeping bags. Remember, what may suit an adult in the depths of winter will certainly be far too hot for a toddler at the height of summer.

For younger toddlers, you may prefer to use baby and toddler sleeping bags rather than blankets. These are quilts that you zip around your baby and through which they can put their arms. There are two advantages: firstly, your toddler will not lose his covers in the middle of the night and become cold, and secondly, as he becomes more agile, it's a great physical deterrent for potential cot escapees. It's almost impossible to climb over cot bars zipped up in a sleeping bag.

NOISE

When your toddler is tired and ready for bed he will sleep – no matter what is going on around him. A very young child can sleep through train noise, being under a flight path, next to a motorway or in a household full of noisy, excitable adults. If this sort of environment is what your child has been used to since he was a baby then there's no reason why you need to turn down the volume now he's a toddler. In fact, if you did, he might actually find the absence of these 'ambient' sounds disturbing. What will wake him up is a startling type of noise like a car horn or an alarm going off, not the hustle and bustle of a busy household.

THE BEDROOM

Your toddler's bedroom needs to be a special place, a very separate space to where he's been hanging out all day, where he's been playing, eating and socialising. It's where he wants to go at the end of each day for a good night's sleep. So try and make it a quiet, restful place, not an indoor adventure playground. Keep his favourite toys of the moment out of his room, or make sure they are packed away in boxes or cupboards each night. That way you avoid late-night impromptu play sessions. Likewise, it's best to keep electronics – TVs, computers, and DVD players – out of the bedroom. Again, they will be tempting for insomniac toddlers but it's also best that young

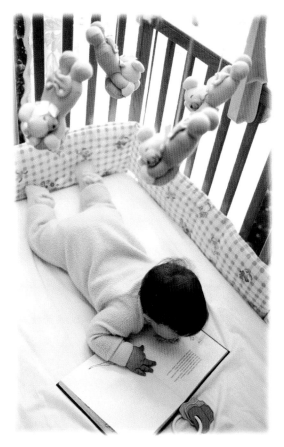

children are supervised when watching television or when using a computer.

Create a bedroom that is nurturing and gentle and that has a bookshelf with lots of bedtime story books, cuddly toys and soft colours. And don't let your toddler's bedroom be a place of punishment, the room in the house he's sent to when he's been naughty and which he comes to associate with being upset.

If your child is scared of the dark then put a night-light in his room, or keep his door slightly open so there's a bit of light coming in from the rest of the house.

ESTABLISHING A GOOD BEDTIME ROUTINE

If your toddler is not in a bedtime routine yet, then now is as good a time as any to start – it is never too late to introduce one.

A bedtime routine is a very natural way to end each day. Once established, as the routine begins your toddler will realise that the pace of the day has changed, and he's now in a wind-down period that will end with him going to sleep. The classic bedtime routine usually begins with a bath, then changing into pyjamas, getting into bed, having a story, a good-night cuddle and then (hopefully) sleep. But everyone's circumstances are different – find out what routine works for you and your toddler, and adapt it as he gets older.

ROUTINE TIPS

● In the beginning implementing a routine is best approached like one big rehearsal. It is an event that will not always run smoothly: on some days you'll want to give it a miss and on other days, despite your best efforts, your toddler may well refuse to sleep. But do persevere – you will get there in the end.

● If you're introducing a routine for the first time then start gradually. Start off by moving into the bedroom area at the same time every day for a few days, and then add a couple more ingredients to the mix like having a bath and reading a story. Gradually your toddler will pick up on these 'cues' signalling that it's time for sleep.

● Choose a quiet month to start your routine. Christmas, birthdays, holidays are probably not the best time – there's far too much going on in their little worlds to appreciate bedtime detail.

Why they work

- Through a regular sequence of events, your toddler will come to associate 'bath, book, bed' with sleep and learn that what starts with moving into the bedroom area will always end with him being put down in his cot or bed for the night.
- It's a very effective way of communicating 'time for bed': that's it, the day is nearly over, no negotiation. This way you avoid many a battle.
- Young children actually thrive on routine – they like to know what's going to happen next, they feel secure with a loosely timetabled existence that varies little from day to day.
- It's the type of routine that anyone can pick up on. A relation, a babysitter or a carer. You don't have to be there to make it happen.
- It's also extremely portable. Even though your toddler may be in a new environment – staying somewhere else for the night – as soon as you kick off the bedtime routine he will understand what's happening.

THE BASICS

- How long should it take? The bedtime routine should be no more than an hour and no less than 30 minutes. Longer than an hour and your toddler may start to wonder when it will end, becoming distracted or cranky; if you try to hurry through the routine, however, he will sense that you're rushing him and this might make him agitated.
- What time should it commence? Decide on a bedtime and work backwards from there – so at least 30 minutes before lights out start your bedtime routine.
- What time for lights out? Most parents opt to put their toddler to bed between seven and seven-thirty in the evening. But this is by no means a given – it's important to do what suits you. If your toddler's needs can be made to fit in with yours and any older children in the family, then the whole

thing will be much easier to pull off. In many European countries children go to bed much later and seem absolutely fine with that. What matters is that your child is getting enough total sleep over a 24-hour period. Perhaps the easiest way of working out a suitable bedtime is to think what time you want your child to wake up in the morning and work backwards from there.

Winding Down

- A change of pace. As soon as your toddler has had his evening meal, slow everything down. All the activities at this time should be low-key; keep stimulation to a minimum. For example, while it's understandable if you or your partner come in from work and want to make a big fuss of your toddler, it may be just at the time when you need him to settle down.
- Don't expect a 'wind down' to bedtime to work if your toddler is not ready for sleep. If he's had a nap late in the day, which has left him refreshed and raring to go, it doesn't matter how good your routine is, it will not work.
- Likewise you don't want your child to be over-tired before you start this routine. It's not for nothing that this time of day is called 'the cranky hour'.
- Change the tone and tempo of your voice. Saying over and over again in a calm and monotonous voice 'time for bed' has a hypnotic effect on children.
- It's hard – but do try not to get cross with your toddler. This will make getting him into bed and off to sleep more difficult. Likewise, don't try to rush him.

THE ROUTINE

- Move to a different area of the home. You want everything associated with the routine to be different from what's gone on before. So keep to the bedroom area.
- Toddlers often say they are hungry before bed. This could be a stalling tactic, but often it's a good couple of hours since they last ate. So a warm drink or healthy bedtime snack will often help them go to sleep. If you don't want a surge of energy and hyperactivity, avoid giving them anything sugary before bed.
- The bath. Young children usually love bathtime. They enjoy playing with their bath toys and the bubbles. It's a very good way of relaxing, and your toddler will find the warm water calming and soothing.
- A book or a puzzle. Reading at bedtime is not only a wonderful way to mark bedtime, it's also a great way of nurturing your toddler's imagination and a love of books. This is a very intimate time between you and your

child, so try not to speed read – take time to discuss the characters and illustrations.

- A lullaby. Young children love to be sung to. It is perhaps the oldest trick in the book to settle a child by singing to him. But if crooning isn't your thing, put on a calming tape or CD to fill the unfamiliar silence.
- Talking things through. This is a lovely time to chat through how the day has gone.
- Cuddle or good-night kiss. A big hug is wonderfully reassuring for a young child, and it's good for you too.

A COMFORTER

If your toddler starts showing an attachment to a favourite piece of sad-looking blanket or a particular soft toy, then that's OK. These 'transitional objects' will help your toddler to sleep without you standing by. He will find it reassuring when he realises that his chosen blanket or teddy will not be going anywhere, that it is staying in his cot next to him all night. Rather than being seen as a babyish trait, 'comforters' enable a toddler to become more independent.

MOVING FROM A COT TO A BED

This is a big event in the life of a toddler, and usually happens some time between 18 months and 3 years. A few bold parents move their child into a bed as early as 15 months, others wait until they are 3½ years old. There are no hard-and-fast rules – it's best done when the time feels right for you all. How well your toddler takes to the transition very much depends on what type of child they are, how attached they are to their cot, and how well you 'sell' the concept.

When it's time to move your toddler into a bed

- Size – your toddler may be too big for the cot he's in, and need a bigger space to move around in at night. Rolling into the sides of the cot while he's asleep wakes him up.
- Safety – he's too mobile for the cot and its sides are no longer the welcome deterrent they once were. He's developed a great abseiling trick down the side and you fear for his safety.

- Necessity – there's another baby on the way that needs the cot, though ensure your toddler is ready to move before you do this.
- Potty training – if you want to teach your toddler to go without nappies, he needs access to a potty or a toilet at all times. A cot may prevent this.
- He wants to – he's seen his big brother sleeping soundly in a bed and he wants to be 'grown-up' like him.

The best ways to do it

- If your child is getting a new bed, make a feature of it. Bring him in on the decision of which one to buy, take him to the shop or sit him on your knee while you browse online.
- If you've got the space, and the patience, keep the new bed and cot going at the same time. That way your toddler won't be rushed into a big change, he can gradually move into the big bed, having the odd night in his old cot when he's scared.
- Start out by using much the same bedding as you had in the cot – the same duvet, sleeping bag or pillow. That way it won't be such a dramatic changeover.

- You could try introducing a reward system such as a star chart. Every time your toddler sleeps in his own bed he gets a star and after a certain number of stars he gets a treat.
- After a night in his bed make a big deal of it. Heap on the praise.
- There's no need to change your toddler's bedtime routine, you want all the same signals to be in place.

Things to watch out for

- Your toddler may initially find this a difficult transition to make. He may be anxious, finding it difficult to settle and waking during the night. He may 'regress' into some bad sleeping habits. Do give him lots of reassurance.
- If another baby is on the way, make sure you move your toddler into his own bed well before the due date. Moving from a cot to a bed takes some effort from you. You will not be able to give it your 100 per cent attention if you've got a newborn to cope with as well. Moving your new baby into your toddler's cot shortly after the birth may increase your toddler's sense of being displaced. It's best to move your toddler out of his cot two months before the baby arrives.

- Your toddler might take advantage of his new-found freedom. He may think it's great he can just roam around his room after lights out – and potentially the rest of the house. If he does make unscheduled appearances, make sure you take him straight back to his new bed (see pages 37–8).

Chapter 3

WHAT YOU CAN DO DURING THE DAY
to help your toddler sleep at night

Most parents know that if their toddler has a 'bad night' – if he has too little sleep or wakes up often – it will affect him the following day, making him tired and irritable. However, what is not so well known is that if your toddler has a 'bad day' – if he doesn't get enough exercise, if he drinks too many sugary drinks or doesn't nap enough – he will have a bad night. What happens to your child during the day affects his sleep during the night – the two are interlinked, so if you want your toddler's nights to go well, have a look at what he's doing with his days.

NIGHT AND DAY

As adults, we take for granted that there is a day time and a night time, and that generally we sleep at night and are awake during the day – what is known as a 'diurnal' sleep pattern. Some children learn the difference as babies; others learn when they are toddlers.

By 12 months old your child will know day and night are not the same – even if he has yet to respect that difference. If you've got a toddler who clearly thinks that the night is for partying and the day for dozing and sleeping in, don't despair – with a bit of tinkering here and there you can 'readjust' the balance.

- To help your toddler respect the difference it's important to be very clear about that difference. Make sure your toddler can see that the day is for eating in, playing, having friends round, watching TV and using up lots of energy. At night it's all change. This is when your toddler needs to be quiet, the lights are down low, there's no snacking, no visitors and no excitement.
- Follow a bedtime routine (see pages 20–23). Even if your toddler only sleeps for a few hours after you've put him to bed for the night, it's a good way of flagging up that the day has ended and the night is beginning.
- Try to keep everything dark at night. If you have to go in to your toddler's room

for a feed or to comfort him, try and do it in darkness, or at least keep the room very dimly lit. This way your toddler will associate 'darkness' with sleeping. You can encourage your child to make this connection during the day by keeping his curtains closed when he goes for a nap, or putting up black-out blinds to keep out bright sunlight.

- Keep interaction with your toddler to a minimum at night. If you go to him try not to engage: don't make eye contact or smile or talk to him.
- Try and spend some time each day outside. Being exposed to natural light helps children sleep better at night.

SLEEP ASSOCIATIONS

What do you associate with going to sleep – a bed, darkness, less noise than during the day? If these conditions are in place you probably fall asleep fairly easily and if none of these conditions change during the night you will probably stay asleep until morning. It's unlikely you will wake up 'in the middle of the night' (or, to be precise, between sleep cycles) because you have learned – probably from when you were a baby or toddler yourself – to get to sleep without help from anybody else.

But what does your toddler associate with going to sleep? Is it lying in a sleepy state in his cot, or is it falling asleep while being cuddled, while holding a bottle, or with you constantly by his side? If this is the case then he will expect this every time he tries to fall asleep – between each sleep cycle – which can happen up to five times a night. So unless you change his sleep associations you could find you are very busy and very tired indeed.

It's easier to try and change these associations during the day – when you are awake and have more energy – than in the middle of the night when all you want to do is sleep. So start off trying to change some of these associations at nap times and bedtime, just before your toddler goes off to sleep.

PHYSICAL AFFECTION

At nap times, and especially at bedtime, when you say good night to your toddler in his cot or bed, it's the time to hug and kiss your child, to make him feel safe, secure and much loved. This is when he'll be tired, cranky and crave physical affection. So cuddle him tight and then tuck him in well. But make sure when it comes to the point of your actual departure – i.e. when you are leaving the room – that your child is actually still awake. Even if it's in a sort of drowsy, slipping-from-consciousness sort of way, it's best your toddler vaguely knows what's going on – that he realises you're leaving, that he's made the connection. If your child associates falling to sleep with being in your arms, or you lying down beside him, then he will expect the same sort of hands-on service every time he wakes up and tries to fall asleep again. And this, as has been explained above, happens many times during the course of one single night.

As a way of reassurance, it's worth remembering that if your child is getting plenty of attention and affection during the day then he doesn't need it throughout the night as well. He will survive absolutely fine without nocturnal hugs and kisses. With the exception of the odd nightmare or night terror, he's best left to get on with the task in hand on his own – that is, sleeping through the night.

So pile it on during the day – it will be of benefit to you as well as your toddler. All young children like to be held and cuddled by the people they know best. Research shows that you will benefit from this contact too. The light touch and gentle pressure that comes from hugging a child causes the release of oxytocin, sometimes called the 'cuddle hormone'. It induces anti-stress effects such as lowering blood pressure, reducing anxiety and pain, and making you feel calm and relaxed. It makes everybody feel good – not just the person getting the hug, but the one giving it as well.

COMFORT FEEDING

Like the rest of us, toddlers need a balanced diet. They need their '5-a-day', five portions of fruit and veg, and the right balance of carbohydrates, protein, fats, vitamins and minerals. Your child will get all this with a varied diet and the best way to make this happen is to introduce him to lots of different tastes and textures from an early age.

If your toddler is getting plenty of the right type of food and drink during the day then there is no need, unless he is sick, for any topping-up at night. Babies as young as six months old are capable of going through the night without being fed, so if your toddler has enough nourishment during the day, and does not go to bed hungry and thirsty, he can easily manage to last from bedtime to breakfast without a drink or a snack.

What may be happening is that your child is seeking a teat or a nipple to suck on more out of comfort than hunger, using it as a means to get off to sleep again. He associates feeding with falling asleep. But giving your child a long drink of milk or orange juice in the middle of the night has a double-whammy effect; not only are you hitting his digestive system in the early hours of the morning with the sugars and proteins, you're also helping to create discomfort through wet nappies.

If you want to break this association then try weaning your child off his night-time feeds.

- Do this gradually, over a period of two weeks or more. You are much less likely to succeed if you stop night-time feeds suddenly.
- Slowly cut down on the length of the feeds by a few minutes each night.
- If your toddler wakes at the same time every night for a feed then make him wait for it. Delay giving him a feed by five minutes or so each night. This will steadily increase the intervals between feeds.
- Gradually replace milk with water.

EXERCISE

Children need to exercise every day. They need it for fitness and for development, so they can put all their recently acquired mobility skills to the test: crawling, walking, climbing and running. Aim for about an hour of moderate exercise a day. This could be a run round the garden, a trip to the park, a walk to the local shops and back. Any trip out of the house for a little person is a major outing; it's an adventure in itself that your child will find fascinating. And plenty of physical exercise during the day will certainly help your child fall asleep easily at night and stay asleep.

ROUTINE, ROUTINE, ROUTINE

Toddlers love it; in fact, they thrive on living by the clock, on knowing when mealtimes are, when to expect a snack, when it's time for nursery, naps and bedtime. Bringing children up in an organised environment helps them know what's going to happen next because they actually don't cope that well with surprises – with unexpected visitors, with missed meals or late nights. That's why ad hoc or out-of-the-ordinary events and arrangements often end in tears.

Therefore, dull as it may seem, toddlers love the reassurance of day following night, lunch following breakfast, and bedtime following teatime. They like everything to be clearly signposted. So in the same way that you are trying to set their night-time clock, you need to work on their daytime one as well. If they eat, rest and play at roughly the same time every day, you are more likely to get them to sleep at the same time every night.

INTRODUCE DAYTIME NAPS

The vast majority of young children need to sleep during the day as well as at night. It helps them function better when they are awake and, surprisingly, helps them to sleep better at night. They are able to fall asleep more easily and stay asleep. An over-tired toddler is more likely to rouse often in his sleep. The signs that your toddler may need a nap – especially in the afternoon – are that he has plenty of energy in the morning, is bright, alert and ready to go, but tires by lunchtime and is clearly flagging in the early afternoon.

Ways of introducing a nap

- Make having a nap an event like bedtime. Your toddler will need the same sort of signals to see that it's time to wind down and sleep. So try a cut-down version of a bedtime routine. Quietly read a book in your toddler's room or play a gentle game, something to flag up it's time to get into his cot and sleep.
- Make sure your toddler has had plenty of activity before his nap time and hasn't had a quick 40 winks to refresh him in the car or his buggy previously – take him out in his buggy or for a drive in the car after his nap and not before. It's surprising what a quick catnap can do for a toddler's short-term energy levels, and how it can affect his ability to fall asleep at the times you want.
- Start by introducing a regular morning waking time as well as a regular bedtime – it will give you a much better chance of making a regular nap time happen each day if you have these in place.

Chapter 4

WHAT YOU CAN DO
to help your toddler sleep well

In the middle of a sleep-deprived haze it may be difficult to believe that you don't need to feel like this — that you and your toddler do not need to wake up several times each night, that he doesn't need to go to bed so late, and that he doesn't need to come into your bed if you don't want him there. The truth is, it is actually possible to change your child's sleep habits, to shape the way he sleeps and stays asleep, to influence his nights. If it suits you, there are ways and means of tinkering around the edges to influence your toddler's sleep patterns and cycles, and there are actions you can take to help the whole family sleep better.

CUTTING BACK ON DAYTIME NAPS

By his first birthday your toddler will still need around 11 hours' sleep a night and one or two naps during the day. However, this is around the time when young children start to drop their morning nap and just have one long nap after lunch each day. Not all toddlers will do this – most aren't ready to go down to one nap a day until they are 18 months, and some will keep their two-a-day habit until their second birthday. You know your child, so you are the best person to decide if he is ready for the next step.

Signs that your toddler is ready to go from two naps to one

- Your toddler is increasingly difficult to settle at nap times; whereas previously he would snuggle down easily and be asleep within minutes, now he uses as many delaying tactics as he can get away with.
- He doesn't appear to tire in the morning. He has plenty of energy, is bright and alert.
- He is difficult to get to sleep at his usual bedtime and he wakes up earlier in the mornings.

Tips for dropping the morning nap

- When you drop your toddler's morning nap, if he is clearly flagging by lunchtime then bring this meal earlier. You could start off by making it as early as 11.30 to 12.00 and putting your toddler to bed straight after lunch for a two-hour afternoon nap. As he gets used to going without his morning nap, gradually push lunchtime back to around 12.30 to 1 p.m. and put him down for his nap after that.

AVERAGE NUMBER OF HOURS OF SLEEP OVER A 24-HOUR PERIOD

Age (months)	Naps per day	Total daytime sleep (hours)
12	1 or 2	2–3
18	1	1½–2½
24	1	1–2
36	0 or 1	0–1½

- Don't let your toddler's last nap of the day be a late one. If he naps too near to bedtime he may not be ready to sleep again so soon. You want about a four-hour difference between the end of his afternoon nap and bedtime.
- When he starts having just one nap a day he may be sleepier in the evenings. Try bringing his bedtime forward until he is used to his new routine. When he seems settled gradually make his bedtime a bit later each day until it is back to its original time.

THE AFTERNOON NAP

Eventually your toddler will stop napping during the day altogether. For most children this happens some time between their third and fourth birthdays, but you may find either your child is ready to forego his final nap as early as during his second year or not until he starts nursery school.

When it comes to giving up this final afternoon nap it can happen quite suddenly. You may notice your toddler has difficulty falling asleep at nap time, or you might put him in his cot or bedroom and find he stays awake for the duration. So if needs be, take the plunge – cut out this final nap.

ENCOURAGING YOUR TODDLER TO STAY IN HIS BED

It's a fine balance, this one. On the one hand you want to encourage your toddler's new-found independence and increased mobility, his ability to toddle, walk and eventually run, his increased dexterity at handling and turning things (including door handles!), and most of all his ability to communicate to you about his likes and dislikes. Which is all great and worthy of celebration during the day, but less so at bedtime and during the night.

So what do you do when he deploys his new skills to resist getting into, and then refusing to stay in bed? It can be, to say the least, extremely tiring putting on an all-singing, all-dancing bedtime routine to get your toddler into bed and then have him appear downstairs ten minutes later.

Some toddlers are very clever at resisting bed. They may develop a whole stage act of tricks in an attempt to spin out their time with you. There's the 'full bladder' trick, the dehydration one, the stomach aches, and the loss of teddy or whatever else is top of the list of comforters that night.

Tips for making your toddler stay in bed

- When you say good night be firm. You want this to be the final bow with no curtain calls. Make sure your child has had a drink, a snack, been to the loo, got his teddy, all well before it's time to turn the lights off.

- If your toddler does come out of his room, quickly walk him back in. Try to interact as little as possible and be quite businesslike about it. If you give him a warm welcome each time he appears he will sense he's on to a good thing.

- Some parents put stair gates in front of their children's bedroom door. These are the type of gates usually used at the top or bottom of stairs to protect young children from climbing up and/or falling down. However, they can be put to good effect on bedroom doors to keep late-night wanderers in. Before long your toddler will get bored of trying to escape from his room.
- With older toddlers you could try 'rewarding' them for staying in bed. Tell your child that if he stays in his own bed for a certain number of nights he can have a treat. Or try a star chart – a star for every undisturbed night. Just make sure you stick by your promises and heap the praise on every time your toddler manages to stay in his own bed all night.

What to do if your toddler repeatedly comes into your bed

If you and your toddler sleep well together in the same bed, and you are happy to take the risk that this may be the start of an ongoing co-sleeping arrangement, then there isn't a problem and you can continue slumbering.

If, however, letting your toddler into your bed will disturb your sleep and you think you would all be better off if he stayed in his own bed, then be firm. Gently walk your toddler back to his bed each time he appears. Initially you may find you are doing a lot of walking up and down corridors in the middle of the night, but he will soon get the message.

Sometimes, however, the rules need to be bent – if a child is sick or has had a nightmare then parents often welcome their toddlers into their bed. Just be careful this occasional occurrence doesn't become a long-term event.

Dealing with bedtime tantrums

One of the main triggers for tantrums is tiredness, which explains why so many happen at bedtime. You're going about your well-planned bedtime routine and then suddenly, from nowhere, your toddler starts having the mother of all tantrums.

Children can start having tantrums from as young as ten months, but they are most common around the age of two. They are mainly caused by a child's frustration that he can't express himself, or he can't understand why he's not getting what he wants. The best way to deal with your child when he is this upset is to try not to let him affect you – don't get angry or upset. Be patient. Your child's fury will eventually abate and although it may be difficult, it's best to carry on as if nothing happened.

If your child is regularly having tantrums at bedtime it may be because he is generally overtired. If this seems the case check that he's getting enough sleep during the day – especially in the early afternoon.

SLEEP TRAINING – Strategies To Help Your Toddler Sleep Through

'Sleep training' is all about trying to teach your child to sleep well without your help, to shape his sleep habits so he doesn't need any assistance from you to get to sleep and stay asleep. It's about seeing if your toddler can make the transition from wakefulness to sleep by himself. In many ways this is as much a test for you as it is for him, because you need to change the way you respond to your toddler.

There has been a lot of passionate debate about whether sleep training is a good or bad thing.

What its supporters say

- Many developmental sleep and medical experts believe whatever short-term upset sleep training may cause the child, it has no harmful long-term effects.
- Experts believe that by using these methods you are actually doing your child a favour because he will learn how to sleep more deeply and peacefully throughout the night. When your child does rouse between sleep cycles he will not wake up fully as he will not associate falling back to sleep again with you.
- It means the whole family can benefit from uninterrupted sleep. Parents suffering from sleep deprivation often say they have much less patience with

their children, they are more prone to losing their temper with them, and are less able to enjoy them. So, advocates of these methods argue that a relatively short amount of 'pain' can actually lead to a lot of long-term gain for everybody.

- It can be very effective – if carried out rigidly, dramatic results may be seen in days.
- Generations of parents have successfully used these techniques on children who have grown up to be normal, happy and healthy individuals.
- Many parents who employ a sleep training strategy often wonder why they didn't try it earlier, such is the change in their daily – and nightly – lives.

Arguments against sleep training

- An increasing minority of experts believe it can harm the child. Leaving a very young child to cry for long periods of time causes them to become stressed, and this in turn can have an effect on brain development.
- It can be very tough on the parent who, while trying to carry out the process, becomes stressed and upset as well.
- If you deny your child comfort at night he may become more attention-seeking during the day.
- If success is limited it can leave parents feeling a failure.
- You need a lot of willpower and energy to carry it out and this is the last thing many over-tired parents feel they have.

What sleep training involves

As long as your toddler is not waking because he is sick, or terrified after a nightmare, or frightened of the dark, then you can introduce these sleep strategies from as young as 6 months old.

There are several different methods of sleep training; think about which technique will suit you and your child best, and whether you will be prepared to see it through. Once you have decided, stick to it – half-hearted attempts will do no good.

Controlled crying

This technique was devised by Richard Ferber, a leading US paediatrician, and is also known as a 'progressive waiting' approach. You are basically leaving your toddler to 'cry it out', but you are constantly going into his room to check on him, so it not just a matter of leaving him to cry all night on his own.

Make sure your toddler is awake when you tuck him up in his cot. Say good night and leave the room. If he cries, go back after three minutes to soothe him, and tuck in his sheets and blankets or sleeping bag. Keep your interaction to a minimum and do not make eye contact. Do not pick him up or take him out of his cot. Say good night again and leave his room. If he continues to cry go back in again after five minutes and go through the same process of tucking him in and soothing him, but not picking him up. If your toddler still hasn't settled himself to sleep then continue to go in at 10 minute intervals until he does so. If your child wakes during the night repeat the exercise, working up once more from 3 to 10 minute intervals. The following night do it all again but increase the interval times to 5, 10 and 12 minutes. On the third night, increase the interval times again by a few minutes and keep doing so for successive nights until your toddler has learned to fall asleep by himself.

Pros: This method can bring results in under a week, sometimes within three days. Some parents swear by it, claiming it changed their lives.

Cons: Some parents find it very tough to pull off. In the initial stages it can be traumatic for both parent and child, which is why many parents find it hard to see it through. Your child may only learn that he needs to cry longer and longer each night until you return. And you may find it's taking 2–3 hours each night.

Repetitive reassurance

This is similar to 'controlled crying' but somewhat gentler in that you can reassure your child when you go back in.

Once you've put your toddler

down, awake in his cot, you leave the room. If he cries, go back into the room immediately, tuck him in again and reassure him. You shouldn't cuddle him or interact with him beyond a few soothing words, but you can keep going into his room as often as you like. Keep this up until he falls asleep and do it every time he wakes up during the night.

Pros: The constant reassurances you give your child make it a less severe approach, and you will also be comforted by this. Seeing a parent at intervals can cut down on how upset your child gets while trying to get to sleep.

Cons: It will probably take longer to be effective – be prepared for at least a week of several hours a night spent going in and out of your child's bedroom a number of times.

Gradual withdrawal

This is a much gentler method, the idea being that you watch your toddler fall asleep.

Once you've settled him in his cot, you sit beside him quietly (you may want to sit and read). At no point do you make eye contact or engage with your child. Over the next few nights, you gradually move further and further away from his cot until you are no longer in his room. The aim is only to move a little at a time – you don't move to the next position until your toddler is ready. You can busy yourself with tidying up the room.

Pros: This is a much more reassuring method for both parent and child – he will learn to settle himself but you can see that he has come to no harm.

Cons: This technique requires a lot of patience, and you must be prepared for the long haul. It may take 2–3 nights in each new position before you can move to the next one., as it is your child who dictates the pace. And it can be upsetting and confusing for some children to have a parent in their room making no attempt to comfort them.

IDEAS FOR COPING WITH TIREDNESS

For your sanity, it's important to find ways of coping with fatigue.

● Sleep when your toddler sleeps. Most toddlers sleep for an average of 11 hours at night (even if they do wake up). This gives you plenty of opportunity to try going to bed early occasionally – or even sleeping in if your toddler does. Likewise with naps – if your toddler snoozes for an hour or two during the day then why don't you join him? Try putting off the long list of chores you have to do in this time you have on your own. Being positive about parenting is half the battle and you are far more likely to feel this if you feel rested.

- If you have a partner, ask them to help with sleep training. Or ask a relative or friend to stay with you and do alternate nights.
- Keep life simple and try not to organise too many things. If you're really tired you won't enjoy them anyway.
- Look after yourself. Eat and exercise well. A healthy balanced diet plus exercise will help your energy levels and make you feel less tired.
- Remember that this period of sleeplessness won't last for ever. Hang in there. Your toddler will eventually learn to sleep through the night, allowing you to as well.

Chapter 5

THINGS THAT MAY GET IN THE WAY
of a good night's sleep

Just when you thought you might be there – you've got your toddler sleeping through the night, going to bed on time, even waking up at roughly the same time each morning – something totally unexpected might come along to knock your child's sleep patterns for six. Don't be disheartened, all your hard work has not gone to waste, nearly all toddler sleep setbacks are temporary – within a few days or weeks everything will be back to what it was.

ILLNESS

All children get ill from time to time, maybe with a cold or a tummy bug. It's estimated that toddlers pick up 7–10 different cold bugs every year. When he's ill your child will seek more reassurance from you, he may be more 'needy', wanting more hugs, closer contact and much soothing. He will seek this both day and night.

Your toddler's symptoms may include loss of appetite, a runny or blocked nose, a cough, slight feverishness, sickness or diarrhoea, all of which will tend to affect his sleep. Although he will sleep more when he's ill, it will be intermittent and not at his usual times. He will probably nap more during the day and not sleep so well at night, waking more frequently than usual. In sleep terms your toddler may well regress – it may feel as if you've got a young baby on your hands again as he wakes up several times during the night needing constant reassurance.

If your child has a blocked nose, it might cause him to wake often during the night. You might as well resign yourself to a few nights of disturbed sleep while he's unwell.

These types of minor illnesses usually last no more than a week, so try not to let them have a lasting impact on any good sleep practices you have established. However, it can be a tough call this one – you don't want to revert to the old ways of when your child was younger, like cuddling him to sleep or letting him fall asleep in your arms, but, if he becomes very distressed while he is ill, he will want, and definitely need, comforting. So use your judgement. For instance, if he's stopped having night feeds, then just give him water to drink if he is thirsty at night. And don't bother trying to introduce or continue with any sleep training technique while your child is sick. Wait until he has fully recovered.

SNORING

It comes as a bit of a surprise to hear a toddler snore. There's your little one curled up in bed with an angelic look on his face, but when you listen closely you realise he's snuffling and snorting away like a steam train.

If your toddler's snoring only happens occasionally and you can link it to a cold or an allergy, then there usually isn't much to worry about. This short-term nasal obstruction doesn't last long and your child will be sleeping quietly again soon.

However, if your toddler's snoring is chronic, and is happening night after night, then he may be diagnosed as having 'obstructive sleep apnoea'. This is where a person's breathing is impaired by narrow air passages. Your toddler may at times sound as if he's gasping for breath, he will probably sleep with his mouth open and wake frequently because of this disturbed breathing.

The most common cause for this in young children is enlarged tonsils and adenoids (glands in the throat just behind the nose). Your child may need a small operation to have these removed. Your GP will advise you.

Occasionally sleep apnoea can be caused by obesity. If your child is very overweight it can cause his airways to be narrowed. Again, your doctor can tell you how best to manage your child's weight and snoring.

TEETHING

Teething affects children differently. Some seem hardly bothered by this stage of their development; others can have a really tough time of it and can be irritable. Teething can cause dribbling, swollen gums, a desire to suck more than usual, and occasionally a slightly raised temperature.

Most children start getting their first teeth as babies – these are canines and appear between five and nine months old. They won't get their first molars, the big, awkward teeth at the back of the gum, until they're toddlers – between 12 and 15 months. Second molars usually appear between 22 and 30 months. These large, flat teeth can take a bit of time coming through and can cause a lot more discomfort. Sucking from a dummy or bottle may be painful as it can make your toddler's gums hurt. So if your toddler uses this as a way to get to sleep, he may find it difficult for a few days.

You can buy soothing gels from your pharmacist to gently rub on to your child's gums, or teething rings your toddler can bite on.

However, it's worth knowing that discomfort from teething will only affect sleep for a few nights, not weeks. So, if the problem persists, you need to look elsewhere for the cause.

FOOD INTOLERANCE

The symptoms of food intolerance vary widely – from eczema and asthma to diarrhoea, to maybe just being a little bit irritable – and tracking down which food might be affecting your child can be tricky. However, all the symptoms have the potential to affect your toddler's sleep. If you think he might have an intolerance or an allergy to something, or you are in any way worried about his reaction to certain foods, consult with your doctor or health visitor immediately.

SEPARATION ANXIETY

Separation anxiety tends to happen in older babies and younger toddlers. It starts at around nine months and lasts several months before it gradually eases.

At around this age babies and toddlers start showing that they don't like it when you are not around. They cry when you leave the room, they are more clingy than usual, they cry if they are picked up by someone unfamiliar – all classic signs of separation anxiety. They literally do not want you out of their sight.

This is a very normal part of your toddler's development – it shows he is becoming more aware of who he is, and who you are, and that there might just be a difference. But there is a possible knock-on effect with regard to his sleeping: if he is disturbed during the night, he may want you there by his side and become distressed if this does not happen fast. Any separation from you – day or night – will cause your toddler anxiety. This calls for patience, because such anxiety may last for several months. If you do not want to be with him every time he settles himself to sleep again, then maybe try a sleep training technique like gradual withdrawal.

You may find signs of separation anxiety return when your toddler starts nursery. Going into a new environment with lots of different people may make him anxious. He may become especially needy at night; again this will pass as he gains confidence in his new surroundings.

NIGHT FEARS

Nearly all children express a fear of the night at some time or other – they are frightened of the dark, think there are monsters under the bed, or that there's someone hiding behind a flapping curtain. Children have very vivid imaginations and the younger they are the more difficult they find it separating fact from fiction. So watch what bedtime stories you read them – the goblin in the fairy book may seem fairly benign before lights out, but when you've said your good-nights and the room is dark, in your toddler's mind the goblin may well take on a life of its own. Likewise, be careful what television or DVDs your toddler watches before bed – certain images may stick in his mind to re-emerge after dark.

These fears may be exacerbated by anxiety over starting a nursery or the arrival of a new baby in the family. What may seem to you like little changes are pretty huge in a toddler's life, so give him plenty of reassurance – his fears are very real.

What to do if your child has night fears

- Listen to his fears and reassure him. You may think it's nothing to worry about but he certainly does.
- Move your toddler's bedtime later so he becomes very sleepy. This will make him fall asleep sooner.
- Put a soft night-light on in your child's bedroom.
- Leave a tape playing with soothing music on.

NIGHTMARES

Nightmares are essentially dreams with unhappy endings – they can start out well but always end badly, giving you a scare. As with all dreams, they occur when we are experiencing REM sleep – usually towards the latter part of the night. They are not very common in children under two years old, so the younger a toddler the less likely they are to have a nightmare.

It's fairly clear when your child is woken by a nightmare – he will wake up fully from his sleep, he will look and act frightened, he may well be in tears and, if he's able to, will recount some of the detail. Very young children have difficulty distinguishing between a dream and reality so will need a lot of comforting and reassurance.

Leaving a night-light on or the door open, lying down beside your toddler or letting him come into your bed will all help calm him down and set him off to sleep again.

SLEEP TERRORS

These can easily be confused with nightmares, but are actually very different.

They happen during non-REM (non-dreaming) sleep when your child is deeply asleep. When your toddler is experiencing a night terror, he is not actually awake, not fully roused. This is why when you go to your child he may look straight through you as if he doesn't know you. He may be crying out, or mumbling, or moaning. If you try to cuddle him he may desperately try to push you away and if he does wake up he won't remember any of it or appear scared.

Some experts believe sleep terrors are more likely to happen if a child is over-tired through not getting enough sleep – during the day as well as the night.

SLEEPWALKING

Like sleep terrors, sleepwalking happens during the deepest stage of sleep – non-REM sleep. Your toddler may appear awake; he may have his eyes open and might even chatter away to you, but he's still very much in a state of sleep and it will be difficult to wake him. If you find your toddler sleepwalking it's best to try and get him back to bed again. Most children tend to grow out of this behaviour.

EARLY RISERS

Just when you thought you were there, after you have successfully moved your toddler from a cot to a bed, have an effective bedtime routine in place and your child is sleeping through the night . . . he starts waking up early.

Reasons for early risers

- Your toddler may be waking a little earlier each day because he is hungry. Try to delay going to him. If you bring breakfast forward, he may start waking even earlier. Make sure he is getting enough to eat during the day.
- An over-tired toddler rarely sleeps well, so make sure he naps enough during the day.
- What time your toddler wakes up will depend to a large extent on when he goes to sleep, so if he has a very early bedtime he's not likely to sleep late in the morning. Keep an eye on how much total sleep your child is getting (see the charts on pages 11 and 36). You may need to put him to bed later, especially as he gets older. If you put a twelve-month-old to sleep at six in the evening you will be lucky if he wakes up much after six the next morning. He's had his full quota of sleep. (Having said all that, with some children it doesn't seem to make much difference what time they go to bed, they will be up with the lark.)
- The early-morning light may be waking your child up. Try putting up some blackout blinds to see if that helps.

WHAT TO DO IF YOUR TODDLER KEEPS WAKING EARLY

Don't feel you have to dash in to your toddler just because you've heard him wake up; wait to see if he's happy on his own for a while or manages to go back to sleep. He may start to burble to himself, or play with some of the toys in his cot to amuse himself while you have an extra half-hour's rest.

With older toddlers sleeping in their own beds, try using a clock. Get a fun alarm clock – one with bunny ears that shoot up or a police siren that whirrs when it's time to get up. Tell your toddler he is not allowed out of his room in the morning until the alarm goes off.

Change your sleep habits and get up earlier as well. You never know, you may find the early morning suits you!

GOING DRY AT NIGHT

Potty training usually happens between 18 and 36 months and, as with all developmental milestones, you can't hurry this one, your child has to be ready for it. Going without nappies for the first time can be traumatic for children – both during the day and the night. If your child has difficulty remembering to get up to go to the toilet at night or is worried about it, if he wets himself frequently, all these things will affect his sleep. He will be nervous about having accidents, which will affect how deeply he sleeps and cause him to wake up more often.

It's important, therefore, to wait until your toddler is ready to go without nappies at night. Remember this is not a race – just because a neighbour's child may be out of them early does not mean it's your toddler's turn. When your child wakes up each morning with a dry nappy, it's usually a good sign that it's time to give it a go – to let your toddler try his nights without nappies.

Chapter 6

SPECIAL AND DIFFERENT CIRCUMSTANCES

A lot of life changes happen in a very short space of time for toddlers. They start nursery, often another baby comes along, and sometimes there's a house move as well to accommodate a growing family. These are pretty big changes for grown-ups, so just imagine how huge they are for young children – to them it appears as if their whole world has been turned upside down. These changes all have an impact; it takes time for toddlers to adjust to their rearranged lives, an adjustment that often affects their behaviour and their sleep.

THE BIRTH OF A SIBLING

It is around toddler age that a sibling often turns up on the scene – most commonly when a first child is between 1½ and 2½ years old, his parents have another baby. The irony is that this is the age when toddlers are really starting to get into their stride, it's when they've worked out how to assert their rights and developmentally are pretty much at the peak of their 'Me, Myself, I' stage.

So it is tough, literally overnight, not to be the centre of attention any more – the arrival of a new baby in the home means your toddler has to share the spotlight. He will feel upstaged and jealous. He may react in several different ways – by showing signs of separation anxiety, by having more tantrums, by sulking, or by regressing – resorting to babyish behaviour. If he's been potty trained he may start wetting himself and demanding nappies, or if you've got him drinking out of a cup he may start asking for a bottle – and your perfect toddler, who up until this point had slept so well, may start to be difficult to get into bed and begin waking during the night.

Your toddler will need lots of reassurance so do go to him when he's upset during the night. Try and keep it brief and businesslike – a long drawn-out affair and you'll end up making it a permanent fixture. But find time during the day to give your toddler attention and affection, such as when the baby is sleeping. Or see if a friend or relative can take your baby out for short walks giving you time alone with your toddler to remind him he hasn't been supplanted.

RETURNING TO WORK

It's in a child's second year that many mothers who haven't yet done so think of returning to work. Give yourself at least two months prior to your return to sort out any sleep problems or introduce a sleep training regime. That way you can get any disturbed nights early on so they won't affect your working day.

If you are already at work when your child develops a sleep problem or you want to try a new routine, start it towards the end of your working week so you have the weekend to recover.

When you have gone back to work be prepared for your child to be clingier at night or to spin out the bedtime hour. It will take time for him to adjust to you not being there all the time, so when you are he'll want to make the most of it.

You need to also be prepared for your reaction to being separated from your child during the day. You may find you are the one drawing out the bedtime hour and being more attentive through the night. If you relish this time with your child and neither of you are adversely affected by it the following day, then enjoy it – many working mothers do.

STARTING NURSERY

Few young children start nursery without the odd tear or display of clinginess. It may not happen on the first day, but after a week or so, when your toddler can predict what's coming next, he may start showing how upset he is at being left in this new environment. He may show signs of classic separation anxiety during the day – and at night. Some children, who've previously been very good sleepers, start waking up more and seeking comfort from their parents. Or, your child might start to have night terrors for the first time. He may become frightened of the dark or insist there's a monster in the cupboard. These are all signs of anxiety brought on by one of the biggest changes in your child's life. It's not surprising he is displaying some of these behaviours. So give him lots of reassurance and comfort, and temporarily bend the night-time rules. His worries will pass. After a few weeks he will see that nursery is not a place to fear and can actually be a lot of fun. In fact, when this happens many parents often discover they have a great sleeper on their hands – their toddler comes back exhausted from nursery and sleeps very well indeed.

TWINS

If your twins are identical, they will probably have very similar sleep patterns and ability to settle. If they are fraternal twins (i.e. non-identical), they will be similar only to the same degree as any pair of siblings – that is to say, probably not similar at all.

One twin might be no trouble at all at bedtime, and sleep through without any problem. The other might take ages to settle, and wake several times during the night for reassurance. Despite these differences, the more alike you can make your twins' sleep schedules, the more easy your life will be (and the more sleep you will get).

- Have a relaxed bedtime routine. It doesn't need to consist of much to start with, just a bath, book and bed, but if you keep it to the same time every day it will help everyone get into the swing of things.
- As with a single child, the sooner they learn to settle themselves, the better, which means keeping the cuddling and comforting before tucking in to a minimum. Try making sure they get into the cots when they are drowsy, before they are in a deep sleep.
- If one (or both) of your toddlers wakes in the night, do not immediately go in. Your twins are used to being around each other and you'll be surprised at how little one of them crying will disturb the other. If his crying becomes less intense, try holding back a bit to see if he will fall asleep on his own.
- It will be much less complicated if your twins go to bed together and get up together, so make sure they are both awake at the same time in the morning – when you want them to be. If you all start your day together there's a much better chance you'll end it together.
- Some parents find it easier when they start sleep training to put one twin in a separate bedroom. However, in some cases, your toddler may not like being in 'unfamiliar' surroundings. You will have to gauge this for yourself.

If you are still experiencing problems, try contacting the Twins and Multiple Births Association (TAMBA) – see page 61 for contact details.

SHARING A BEDROOM

Children relatively close in age usually enjoy sharing a bedroom. They enjoy the camaraderie and find it comforting having someone else in their room. But if siblings are sharing a bedroom and one has sleep problems, it's often easier to separate them at night if you are going to introduce any form of sleep training.

Move the better sleeper to another room, or into your room temporarily, until the problem is sorted.

TODDLERS WHO NEED EXTRA HELP TO SLEEP

In some circumstances the normal sleep strategies described so far may not be effective or may take longer to work. You may need extra help and support, and in some cases specialist help. If your child has a persistent sleep problem, it is best to seek professional guidance as early as possible.

A toddler with a disability or a challenging condition

Some disabilities or conditions may cause or add to sleep problems, and in many cases trying to adopt good sleeping habits through sleep training may be unrealistic or inappropriate. Also, parents may be reluctant to encourage practices such as controlled crying with such vulnerable children. But that's not to say you shouldn't try to adopt some basic good practice. You may find your toddler really benefits from routine and schedules. Ask your GP or health visitor for advice – it's best to get specialist advice on the practicality of implementing one of these routines on a strict basis.

Your toddler may have difficulty learning from experience, recognising sleep cues and routines, or even knowing the difference between day and night. Keep trying, but be prepared for setbacks.

Toddlers diagnosed with autistic spectrum disorders can have trouble settling down to sleep, may wake up frequently, and will be more likely to wake early in the morning. It's best to seek professional advice.

If your child has Down's syndrome he may have breathing difficulties, which will affect sleep. Your health visitor will advise you on what to do or you could seek support from a specialist organisation.

The sleep cycles and patterns of a toddler suffering from brain damage may be affected. He may need medication to help him. Your doctor and health visitor will be able to advise you on how to help your child, or you could contact a specialist sleep clinic.

MOVING HOUSE

If you find moving house stressful and disorientating, just think how very young children find it. They may initially think it exciting, but when it dawns on them that they are going to have to pack up their bedroom to go somewhere strange and new, they may not think it such a great idea.

So when you get into your new house make it a priority to try and set up your toddler's bedroom for his first night in his new home. It does not have to be anything elaborate, it just helps if there are a few familiar things in his room, like his bed, or some soft toys, or even just his bedding. At bedtime play the bedtime lullaby CD he's familiar with, read his favourite storybook – in other words, try and stick to your usual bedtime routine. Even if the rest of the house is just a collection of packing boxes, try to make your child's sleeping area as cosy as possible. That way you're more likely to get him to sleep and to stay asleep.

However, the first night in a new home is always going to be a bit of a write-off. Sleep experts warn of 'first-night syndrome'; that it takes this long to settle into new surroundings. We all need time to adjust to a new sleeping environment – to the difference in light, noise, type of bed or mattress, to the position of the bed. This sleep blip is temporary though – assuming there's no time-zone change, by the second or third night 'rapid habituation' should have occurred, and you and your toddler should all be snoring sweetly.

DIFFERENT TIME ZONES AND CHANGING CLOCKS

Wherever you are, even if it's the other side of the world, try starting your toddler off on local time straight away. It might take him a few days to make the switch, or as much as a week in some time zones, but then again you might find that he makes the 'switch' quicker than you.

Likewise, when the clocks are switched from winter to summer time, and vice versa, it's best to start your toddler off at his new bedtime straight away. Most children manage to adjust to the hour's difference within a week.

Conclusion

In the end we all get there – most children grow into adolescents and adults who sleep through the night in their own bed. Give it a bit of time and your child will also get there – he will eventually pick up the 'falling back to sleep easily' trick, lose his fear of the dark, put himself to bed and not get up when the sun rises. The long-term goal is not the problem – it's how quickly you want to get there, and how long are you prepared to wait for all this to happen.

If you're not in a hurry then just sit back and wait for nature to take its course. However, the toddler years are very precious ones – it's when your child really starts to develop his personality, assert his independence and begin to get to grips with life. If lack of sleep is preventing you and your toddler from enjoying this time then by helping him to sleep you will be doing both of you a huge favour.

USEFUL ADDRESSES

The Association for Post-Natal Illness
145 Dawes Road, Fulham
London, SW6 7EB
Helpline: 020 7386 0868
Website: www.apni.org
Provides support to mothers
suffering from post-natal illness and
works towards increasing public
awareness of the illness.

*Association of Breastfeeding
Mothers (ABM)*
PO Box 207, Bridgwater
Somerset, TA6 7YT
Counselling hotline: 08444 122949
Website: http://abm.me.uk
A mutual support group for
breastfeeding mothers. Puts
mothers in touch with each other
and provides information and advice.

Contact a Family
209– 211 City Road, London, EC1V 1JN
Phone: 020 7608 8700
Fax: 020 7608 8701
Helpline: 0808 808 3555 or
Textphone: 0808 808 3556
Freephone for parents and families
(Mon– Fri 10am– 4pm and Mon
5.30pm– 7.30pm)
E-mail: info@cafamily.org.uk
Website: www.cafamily.org.uk
There are several parent support
organisations for parents of children
with specific conditions like autism or
Down's syndrome. Contact a Family
provides up-to-date information and
contacts for these various
organisations as well as giving
support and advice to parents of all
disabled children. The charity puts
families in contact with each other
both on a local and national level.

Cry-sis
BM Cry-sis
London, WC1N 3XX
Phone: 08451 228669
Website: www.cry-sis.org.uk
Cry-sis is a charity providing self-
help and support to families with
excessively crying, sleepless and
demanding babies and toddlers.

*Foundation for the Study of Infant
Deaths (FSID)*
Artillery House,11– 19 Artillery Row
London, SW1P 1RT
Helpline: 020 7233 2090 (Mon– Fri
9am– 11pm; Weekends and bank
holidays 6pm– 11pm)
Website: www.fsid.org.uk
FSID offers support and education
to parents and professionals on
reducing the risk of Sudden Infant
Death Syndrome (SIDS).

Gingerbread
307 Borough High Street
London, SE1 1JH
Phone: 0800 018 5026
Website: www.gingerbread.org.uk

Gingerbread is there for lone-parent families. The organisation provides support services and a self-help network to ensure these families do not have to face challenges alone.

Home-Start

2 Salisbury Road, Leicester
Leicestershire, LE1 7QR
Phone: 0116 233 9955
Fax: 0116 233 0232
Email: info@home-start.org.uk
Website: www.home-start.org.uk/
The idea behind Home Start is parents supporting parents. The organisation has a network of 15,000 trained parent volunteers who support parents struggling to cope for a variety of different reasons: post-natal illness, disability, bereavement, the illness of a parent or child, or social isolation.

Meet-A-Mum Association (MAMA)

Helpline: 0845 120 3746 (Mon–Fri 7pm–10pm)
Website: www.mama.co.uk
Provides friendship and support to all mothers and mothers-to-be, especially those feeling lonely or isolated after the birth of a baby or moving to a new area. By attending a local MAMA group, mums become part of a network of women wanting to make new friends and support each other through good times and bad.

The National Childbirth Trust

Alexandra House, Oldham Terrace
Acton, London, W3 6NH
Enquiry phone line: 0870 444 8707 (Mon–Thurs 9am–5pm; Fri 9am–4pm)
Email: enquiries@nct.org.uk
Pregnancy and Birth line: 0870 444 8709 (Mon–Fri 10am–8pm)
Breastfeeding line: 0870 444 8708 (Mon–Sun 9am–6pm)
Website: www.nct.org.uk
Provides support for pregnancy, birth and early parenthood. It runs ante-natal classes and post-natal discussion groups as well as providing breast-feeding support.

Parentline Plus

520 Highgate Studios
53-79 Highgate Road, Kentish Town
London, NW5 1TL
Phone: 0808 800 2222
Website: www.parentlineplus.org.uk/
A national charity that works for, and with, parents.

TAMBA (Twins and Multiple Births Association)

2 The Willows
Gardner Road
Guildford, GU1 4PG
Phone: 0800 1380509
Website: www.tamba.org.uk
A nationwide UK charity providing information and mutual support networks.

INDEX

1 3 5 7 9 10 8 6 4 2

Published in 2009 by Vermilion, an imprint of Ebury Publishing

Ebury Publishing is a Random House Group Company

.The Random House Group Limited Reg. No. 954009

Addresses for companies within the Random House Group can be found at www.rbooks.co.uk

A CIP catalogue record for this book is available from the British Library

The Random House Group Limited supports The Forest Stewardship Council (FSC), the leading international forest certification organisation. All our titles that are printed on Greenpeace approved FSC certified paper carry the FSC logo. Our paper procurement policy can be found at www.rbooks.co.uk/environment

Printed and bound in Singapore by Tien Wah Press

ISBN 978 0 09 192909 1

Copies are available at special rates for bulk orders. Contact the sales development team on 020 7840 8487 for more information.

To buy books by your favourite authors and register for offers, visit www.rbooks.co.uk

Please note that conversions to imperial weights and measures are suitable equivalents and not exact

The information given in this book should not be treated as a substitute for qualified medical advice; always consult a medical practitioner. Neither the author nor the publisher can be held responsible for any loss or claim arising out of the use, or misuse, of the suggestions made or the failure to take medical advice.